Great Women in History

Maria Mitchell

by Anna Butzer

Content Consultant: Noel M. Swerdlow,
Professor Emeritus, Astronomy and Astrophysics, History
The University of Chicago

Consulting Editor: Gail Saunders-Smith, PhD

CAPSTONE PRESS
a capstone imprint

Pebble Books are published by Capstone Press,
1710 Roe Crest Drive, North Mankato, Minnesota 56003.
www.capstonepub.com

Library of Congress Cataloging-in-Publication Data
Butzer, Anna.
Maria Mitchell / by Anna Butzer.
     pages cm. — (Pebble books. Great women in history)
  Summary: "Inspire readers with these simple yet comprehensive biographies of some
of history's most courageous women. Carefully leveled text and historically accurate
photographs combine to create an excellent learning experience"— Provided by
publisher.
  Includes bibliographical references and index.
  Audience: Grades K–3.
  ISBN 978-1-4914-0539-0 (library binding)— ISBN 978-1-4914-0542-0 (pbk.) —
  ISBN 978-1-4914-0545-1 (ebook PDF)
  1. Mitchell, Maria, 1818–1889—Juvenile literature. 2. Women astronomers—
United States—Biography—Juvenile literature. 3. Astronomers—United States—
Biography. I. Title.
  QB36.M7B87 2015
  520.92—dc23 [B]   2013047337

Photo Credits
Corbis/Bettmann, 14; Courtesy of the Nantucket Maria Mitchell Association, 4, 6, 8, 12,
16, 18; Getty Images/NYPL, 20; Library of Congress, 10; North Wind Picture Archive,
cover; Shutterstock, cover illus.

Note to Parents and Teachers

The Great Women in History set supports national curriculum standards for social
studies related to people and culture. This book describes and illustrates Maria Mitchell.
The images support early readers in understanding the text. The repetition of words and
phrases helps early readers learn new words. This book also introduces early readers
to subject-specific vocabulary words, which are defined in the Glossary section. Early
readers may need assistance to read some words and to use the Table of Contents,
Glossary, Read More, Internet Sites, and Index sections of the book.

Printed in the United States of America in Stevens Point, Wisconsin.
032014   008092WZF14

Table of Contents

Meet Maria 5

Young Maria 7

Grown-Up Maria 11

Later in Life 17

Glossary 22

Read More 23

Internet Sites 23

Critical Thinking Using the
Common Core 24

Index 24

1818

born

Meet Maria

Maria (Ma-RYE-uh) Mitchell

was the first female

American astronomer.

She discovered a comet.

Maria was born in 1818

on Nantucket Island

in Massachusetts.

 Maria's home on Nantucket Island

1818

born

Young Maria

Maria and her father
shared a love of the stars.
They watched the night sky
together with a telescope.
At age 12, Maria helped
her father predict a
solar eclipse.

 Maria and her father, William

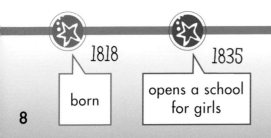

1818

born

1835

opens a school
for girls

Maria's parents believed
in education for girls, not
just boys. This belief was
unusual at the time.
In 1835, at age 17, Maria
opened her own school
for girls.

 Maria (second from left) and her sisters

ATHENEUM

1818
born

1835
opens a school
for girls

1836
becomes a
librarian

Grown-Up Maria

In 1836 Maria started a
job as a librarian. In the
daytime, she studied
math and languages.
At night, she watched
the sky.

 Maria worked at a library called the
Nantucket Atheneum.

1818 born

1835 opens a school for girls

1836 becomes a librarian

1847 discovers a comet

One night in 1847, Maria saw a comet through her telescope. She was the first person ever to see this comet. It was named for Maria. People called it Miss Mitchell's comet.

 Maria using her telescope

1818 born

1835 opens a school for girls

1836 becomes a librarian

1847 discovers a comet

Maria became famous for her discovery. The king of Denmark gave her a gold medal. In 1848 she was the first woman elected to the American Academy of Arts and Sciences.

1848

joins American Academy of Arts and Sciences

1818
born

1835
opens a school
for girls

1836
becomes a
librarian

1847
discovers a
comet

Later in Life

In 1856 Maria left her
library. The next year,
she traveled in the United
States and Europe.
She met other famous
astronomers there.

 Maria in about 1860

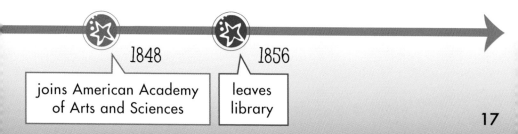

1848
joins American Academy
of Arts and Sciences

1856
leaves
library

1818	1835	1836	1847
born	opens a school for girls	becomes a librarian	discovers a comet

In 1865 Maria became
the first professor at
Vassar College for women.
She and her students
watched the night sky.
"We are women studying
together," Maria said.

 Maria with her students at Vassar College

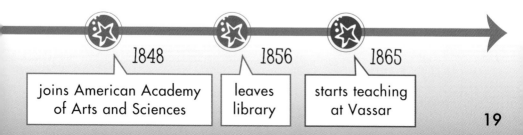

1848
joins American Academy
of Arts and Sciences

1856
leaves
library

1865
starts teaching
at Vassar

1818
born

1835
opens a school
for girls

1836
becomes a
librarian

1847
discovers a
comet

Maria died in 1889. But she lives on in the night sky. A comet, an asteroid, and a crater on the moon are named after Maria.

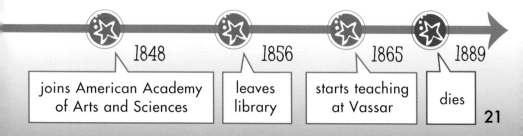

Maria (left) and her assistant at Vassar in 1888

1848	1856	1865	1889
joins American Academy of Arts and Sciences	leaves library	starts teaching at Vassar	dies

Glossary

asteroid—a large space rock that moves around the sun; asteroids are too small to be called planets

astronomer—a scientist who studies stars, planets, and other objects in space

comet—a ball of rock and ice that circles the sun

crater—a large hole in the ground caused by crashing rocks

discover—to see something for the first time

elect—to choose someone as a leader by voting

professor—a teacher with the highest teaching position at a college

solar eclipse—a period of daytime darkness when the moon passes between the sun and earth

telescope—a tool people use to look at objects in space; telescopes make objects look closer than they really are

Read More

Hughes, Catherine D. *First Big Book of Space.* National Geographic Little Kids. Washington, D.C.: National Geographic, 2012.

Hunter, Nick. *Comets.* The Night Sky: And Other Amazing Sights. Chicago: Heinemann Library, 2013.

Ready, Dee. *Librarians Help.* Our Community Helpers. Mankato, Minn.: Capstone Press, 2013.

Internet Sites

FactHound offers a safe, fun way to find Internet sites related to this book. All of the sites on FactHound have been researched by our staff.

Here's all you do:

Visit *www.facthound.com*

Type in this code: 9781491405390

Check out projects, games and lots more at
www.capstonekids.com

Critical Thinking Using the Common Core

1. When Maria was a teacher, what did she teach? Who were her students? (Key Ideas and Details)

2. Why did Maria become famous? (Integration of Knowledge and Ideas)

Index

American Academy of Arts and Sciences, 15
astronomer, 5, 17
awards and honors, 15
birth, 5
comet, 5, 13, 21
death, 21
librarian, 11, 17
Nantucket Island, 5
parents, 7, 9
professor, 19
solar eclipse, 7
telescope, 7, 13
travels, 17
Vassar College, 19

Word Count: 244
Grade: 1
Early-Intervention Level: 21

Editorial Credits
Nikki Bruno Clapper, editor; Terri Poburka, designer; Kelly Garvin, media researcher; Tori Abraham, production specialist